HOW TO FACE LIFE'S UNCERTAINTY?

*Finding Hope in a
Confusing World*

NORMAN WARREN

BARBOUR
PUBLISHING, INC.
Uhrichsville, Ohio

Text copyright © 1988 Norman Warren. Original edition published in English under the title *A Certain Faith* by Lion Publishing plc, Oxford, England. Copyright © Lion Publishing plc 1988.

This edition copyright © 2000 by Barbour Publishing, Inc.

ISBN 1-57748-817-2

All rights reserved. No part of this publication may be reproduced or transmitted in any form or by any means without written permission of the publisher.

All Scripture quotations are taken from the HOLY BIBLE: NEW INTERNATIONAL VERSION® NIV®. Copyright © 1973, 1978, 1984 by International Bible Society. Used by permission of Zondervan Publishing House. All rights reserved.

Published by Barbour Publishing, Inc., P. O. Box 719, Uhrichsville, Ohio 44683 http://www.barbourbooks.com

Member of the
Evangelical Christian
Publishers Association

Printed in the United States of America.

CONTENTS

A CERTAIN FAITH?

There are so many millions of people, how can God possibly be interested in me?'

I'm just a tiny cog in a huge machine—I don't matter.

God seems to be so far away. How can I know He loves me?

I hear people talking about God being with them. How can I know He is with me in my daily life?

I cannot even forgive myself, how can I know God forgives me?

The day of judgment, and death itself, fill me with fear.

How can I be sure death isn't the end?

How can I know there is life beyond the grave?

Will I go to heaven when I die?

You cannot be sure about anything anymore.

These questions, and others like them, come to most people at one time or another. They can cause a lot of worry and unhappiness.

World events, the threat of nuclear explosions, the seeming silence and inactivity of God, all fill many with fear and uncertainty.

Others see the Bible being attacked, ridiculed, and discredited, and ask themselves if they can trust it any longer.

Some feel that it is proud and presumptuous to say you can know God and have eternal life. Can we really be sure?

It is quite possible for you to believe in God, be baptized, and even attend church, and yet not to be able to say definitely you are a Christian. Some days you feel you are, other days you just do not know. You try to live up to God's standards and hope all will turn out all right in the end, but you really don't know.

Deep down you long to have an inner certainty that you are forgiven and belong to God, and to know God's love in your life.

HOW DO I KNOW
GOD LOVES ME?

Creation tells me that God loves me.
Just look around at the world that God has made. See the amazing beauty and color, the care for detail, from the vastness of space and the wonder of the night sky to the restless sea, the soaring mountains to the gentleness of the hills and valleys, the design of a snowflake to the lumbering elephant, the intricacy of eye, ear, and brain.

All this shows God's care for His world. We are part of His creation. He sends the sun and rain, He gives the fruitfulness of the earth, the riches of plant, insect, and minerals, whether we acknowledge Him or not.

The coming of Jesus tells me that God loves me.

I can get some idea of the Creator by studying creation, just as I can learn something of Bach by studying his music. But it all remains rather vague. God does reveal Himself in His creation. But His perfect revelation came when

6

He sent His Son Jesus Christ to be born into our world. That is the greatest proof of God's love.

"For God so loved the world that he gave his one and only Son, that whoever believes in him shall not perish but have eternal life."

JOHN 3:16

Jesus lived in a real place—in occupied Palestine—in real history, for about thirty-three years. The story is told from four different perspectives in the books we know as the Gospels, in the Bible.

As we see Jesus' loving acceptance of all people, no matter what their background, their intellect, or their character, we see God's love in action. In His teaching He likened Himself to a shepherd, the Good Shepherd, who knows His sheep by name, cares for them, and is willing to die for them.

The Bible tells me that God loves me.

The Bible is full of God's love for all people. It is packed with promise after promise of how much God cares for us.

The LORD appeared to us in the past, saying: "I have loved you with an everlasting love."
                                                    JEREMIAH 31:3

In the book of Hosea, there is a beautiful, intimate picture of God's love even for those who do not acknowledge it.

"When Israel was a child, I loved him, and out of Egypt I called my son. But the more I called Israel, the further they went from me. They sacrificed to the Baals and they burned incense to images. It was I who taught Ephraim to walk, taking them by the arms; but they did not realize it was I who healed them. I led them with cords of human kindness, with ties of love; I lifted the yoke from their neck and bent down to feed them."
                                                    HOSEA 11:1–4

GOD'S WORD, THE BIBLE

Can I really trust the Bible? Is it true?

The word Bible comes from a Greek word *biblia* which means "books." The Bible is not one book but sixty-six books. It took about 1,500 years to be completed and was written by about forty people. Among them were kings, a prime minister, a doctor, a tax official, fishermen, and a farmer. Most of the writers never met the other writers. Yet through the Bible there runs an amazing unity and agreement. What is the explanation?

God spoke through the Bible's writers. Through their personalities, their different styles, through their actual words He guided them to write down His words. They did not just sit down and write a book about God. Again and again we have the words, "Thus says the Lord," or "The word of the Lord came to. . . ." The apostle Peter put it like this:

For prophecy never had its origin in the will of man, but men spoke from God as they were carried along by the Holy Spirit.
2 PETER 1:21

Paul summed it up:

All Scripture is God-breathed.

2 TIMOTHY 3:16

The Bible tells us what God is like, and how we can know Him. Without it we would know next to nothing about Him. We would have no idea why we are here or where we are going.

The Bible is packed full of God's promises to His people.

The trouble with some people is that they do not read their Bible to find out these promises. Instead of relying on God's word, they rely on their own feelings or ideas. If you are tired or ill, if you have troubles and worries at home or at work, you may not feel God is with you and loves you. Don't rely on your feelings which change.

Let the Bible be your guide through life.

Your word is a lamp to my feet and a light for my path. PSALM 119:105

Let the Bible keep you from sin.

> *I have hidden your word in my heart that I might not sin against you.*   PSALM 119:11

Let the Bible strengthen your faith.

> *Consequently, faith comes from hearing the message, and the message is heard through the word of Christ.*   ROMANS 10:17

Let the Bible build you up in the Christian life.

> *"Now I commit you to God and to the word of his grace, which can build you up and give you an inheritance among all those who are sanctified."*   ACTS 20:32

Let the Bible give you a confident faith.

> *I write these things to you who believe in the name of the Son of God so that you may know that you have eternal life.*
> 1 JOHN 5:13

GOD KNOWS ALL ABOUT YOU

There are so many people in the world, how can God possibly love me?

We sometimes have a picture of God rather like a harassed telephone operator, desperately trying to connect all the calls that are flooding in. God is not a very big human. He is far, far greater than our tiny, finite minds can ever take in. He has perfect knowledge of everything, of everyone. He knows all about you. The psalmist recognized this in one of the most beautiful of all Psalms:

> O LORD, you have searched me and you
> know me. You know when I sit and when I
> rise; you perceive my thoughts from afar.
> You discern my going out and my lying
> down; you are familiar with all my ways.
> Before a word is on my tongue you know it
> completely, O LORD. You hem me in—
> behind and before; you have laid your hand
> upon me. Such knowledge is too wonderful
> for me, too lofty for me to attain. For you

created my inmost being; you knit me together in my mother's womb. My frame was not hidden from you when I was made in the secret place. PSALM 139:1–6, 13, 15

We see from the life of Jesus, too, God's care for and interest in the individual. Jesus was always ready to spare time with a person, no matter who they were nor what they had done—a proud Pharisee, an immoral woman, lepers and outcasts, sad and lonely people, ordinary people— He accepted them all.

He is interested in us as individuals. We are of infinite worth to Him, so much that He died for us. That is how much value we are to Him. He knows everything about us, the worst as well as the best, and loves us just the same.

"I have summoned you by name; you are mine. Since you are precious and honored in my sight, and because I love you, I will give men in exchange for you, and people in exchange for your life." ISAIAH 43:1, 4

A NEW RELATIONSHIP

A Christian is not someone who just does religious things. Going to church no more makes you a Christian than going to a zoo makes you a chimpanzee.

A Christian is someone who belongs to Jesus Christ; Christ's man, Christ's woman. A Devonian is someone who loves Devon and who belongs there. So a Christian is someone who loves Christ, who belongs to Christ, someone who has let the living Christ enter his or her life to be Lord. For Jesus not only lived in real history. He died, too—and was raised from death to new life.

Some years ago I visited a refugee camp in South Austria. All year round people were streaming over the Yugoslav frontier into Austria. I remember a young Hungarian woman who had watched her parents die of starvation. She decided to make a break for freedom. She crossed at the Austrian frontier and was given a visa stamped with the exact time and place she entered her new country.

I met a young Russian who determined to leave the horrors of Communist oppression. His escape through Poland, Czechoslovakia, and Yugoslavia was a thriller. Finally he crossed the Karavanken mountains into the freedom of Austria. He did not know when he crossed the frontier; he just kept pressing on until he reached an Austrian village and safety.

These two people had this in common: They knew they were free, they were in a new country with a new language to learn, new friends to make, and a new government to obey. All was not going to be easy, but they knew they were free.

In the same way, tired of the dictatorship of sin and disillusioned by the emptiness of life, we long for a new life. We acknowledge our sin, we "repent," we turn our back on it. We commit our lives to Jesus Christ, we ask Him to take over our lives.

Some know the exact moment they crossed the frontier to this new life. Some cannot be sure of the precise moment or day. The important thing is not when, but that you know now.

For the Christian, the new country is the kingdom of God. For the Christian, the new government is the rule of Christ. This is how the apostle Paul put it:

Therefore, if anyone is in Christ, he is a
new creation; the old has gone, the new has
come!   2 CORINTHIANS 5:17

Have you put your trust in Jesus? Have you
accepted Him into your life as Lord? Then you
are in His kingdom, in His care. You are a
Christian. You belong to Him for eternity.

CHOSEN TO BELONG TO HIM

The trouble with many Christians is that
they think it all depends on them. They
hear the good news of Jesus and accept Him—
they decide for Jesus. It's their choice, their deci-
sion. Nothing could be further from the truth. It
is God's doing. Faith is depending on Him, not
on ourselves. God makes all the moves. Long
before you were born He knew all about you.
Years before you ever gave God a thought He
knew you and chose you to belong. This is something we find so hard to grasp. Paul put it like this:

For he chose us in him before the creation of the world to be holy and blameless in his sight. In love he predestined us to be adopted as his sons through Jesus Christ, in accordance with his pleasure and will.

EPHESIANS 1:4–5

He knew you would respond to His love. His Holy Spirit had been at work in you even before your birth, leading you closer to Christ. We are not robots. God does not force anyone to believe. He honors our will, for that is what makes us human beings, with the ability to choose.

Jesus likened Himself to a shepherd going after the lost sheep until He found it. It is only as we look back over our lives that we can see how wonderfully God has been at work—guiding and protecting us, sending that person at that moment to be God's messenger, putting that book into our hands, causing us to go and hear that speaker, even allowing a seeming tragedy to happen that made us to turn to Him for help.

Jesus summed it up so simply:

"You did not choose me, but I chose you."

JOHN 15:16

The emphasis is on Him choosing us; we respond to His love. It brings home to us that our salvation is all of His love and grace and totally undeserved on our part. It destroys all our pride as we realize it is all His doing.

As we grasp this, just how precious each Christian is to Christ, it gives a great inner peace, and an assurance that He will most certainly look after His own.

My sheep listen to my voice; I know them, and they follow me. I give them eternal life, and they shall never perish; no one can snatch them out of my hand.

JOHN 10:27–28

ADOPTED INTO HIS FAMILY

One of our children is adopted. He was born in Saigon in Vietnam toward the end of the war. He was left at an orphanage door with no name, no known parentage—just wrapped up in a piece of cloth.

He was chosen by us, set apart for us, given our name and, after eighteen months, legally adopted into our family. He didn't know what was going on; he was too young and confused. He was loved and accepted long before he could make any response. He has exactly the same rights as our other children, an heir to all we have. There is absolutely no difference in any way in his status and relationship in our family from the natural children.

This picture of adoption is used in the Bible to show the status of the Christians in God's family.

For you did not receive a spirit that makes you a slave again to fear, but you received the Spirit of sonship. And by him we cry, "Abba, Father." ROMANS 8:15

Paul uses for "father" the intimate word "Daddy!"

By trusting in Jesus we become not just children in His family, but legally recognized heirs as well.

Jesus is the Son and heir. We, too, become joint heirs with Him and will possess all the blessings and rights and inheritance that He keeps for His people. "Your Father has been pleased to give you the kingdom," said Jesus (Luke 12:32). Long before we knew anything about Christ, long before we responded, His love was upon us; we were chosen and set apart to belong in His family and to share with Christ the glorious inheritance that belongs to all the children of God. Princes and princesses of God's kingdom—that is what we are in Christ!

Peter was so excited by the prospect that he wrote:

Praise be to the God and Father of our Lord Jesus Christ! In his great mercy he has given us new birth into a living hope through the resurrection of Jesus Christ from the dead, and into an inheritance that can never perish, spoil or fade—kept in

heaven for you, who through faith are
shielded by God's power until the coming of
the salvation that is ready to be revealed in
the last time.　　　　1 PETER 1:3–5

Look through these verses again and mark the
promises. Turn them into a prayer of praise and
thanksgiving.

ACCEPTED AS YOU ARE

This is the cornerstone of the Christian faith.
You do not have to become good before
God accepts you. If that were so, none of us
would ever be Christians. He accepts us not
because of anything in us, anything we have done,
but only because of Jesus—who He is and what
He has done for us. If it all depended upon us, we
would forever be full of doubts. Because it all
depends upon Him, we can be absolutely certain
that we are fully accepted into His family.

A man called Martin Luther discovered this
way back in the sixteenth century. He longed for

peace with God. To find it, he tried everything the church could offer—penances, priesthood, endless prayers, long pilgrimages. He still could not find peace. In fact, he became more guilt-ridden and depressed.

It was when he was studying Paul's letter to the Romans that light dawned on him. He had already seen Christ's suffering in the Psalms: "My God, my God, why have You forsaken Me?" (Psalm 22:1). Martin, too, felt this deep separation from God. But then in Romans he saw that Christ's suffering and death were for human sin—his. Christ had died for Martin's sin.

Jesus took the full weight of God's holy anger towards sin in our place. God declares us, the guilty sinners, "just," because Jesus, the innocent one, out of pure love suffered the consequences of our sin. We are justified in God's sight by faith in Christ and His death for us: justified—just-as-if-I-died.

Jesus died in my place, for my sin. For Martin Luther, this was a fresh discovery. As he grasped this and put his whole trust in his Savior Jesus, he wrote, "I felt myself to be reborn and to have gone through open doors into paradise.

The whole of Scripture took on a new meaning. Whereas 'the justice of God' had filled me with hate, now it became to me inexpressibly sweet in greater love."

Jesus was cut off from His Father so that we might enter into His love. He was rejected that we might be accepted. He took our sin and guilt that we might be forgiven. He died that we might live. If God Himself declares us acquitted from all our guilt, how dare we question it? When God's word tells me this, how can I question it?

When God sees me, He now sees Christ in me. How can I doubt? I can only accept it gladly, humbly, and thankfully. This is how Paul sums it up:

What, then, shall we say in response to this? If God is for us, who can be against us? He who did not spare his own Son, but gave him up for us all—how will he not also, along with him, graciously give us all things? Who will bring any charge against those whom God has chosen? It is God who justifies. Who is he that condemns? Christ Jesus, who

*died—more than that, who was raised to
life—is at the right hand of God and is also
interceding for us. Who shall separate us from
the love of Christ? Shall trouble or hardship
or persecution or famine or nakedness or dan-
ger or sword? As it is written: "For your sake
we face death all day long; we are considered
as sheep to be slaughtered." No, in all these
things we are more than conquerors through
him who loved us. For I am convinced that
neither death nor life, neither angels nor
demons, neither the present nor the future,
nor any powers, neither height nor depth, nor
anything else in all creation, will be able to
separate us from the love of God that is in
Christ Jesus our Lord.*   ROMANS 8:31–39

HE FORGIVES ALL YOUR SINS

One of the results of sin is to cut us off from
God. It is our doing, not God's. Nothing evil
can exist in His presence, any more than darkness

can coexist with light. This is why it seems as if our prayers get no further than the ceiling.

The trouble with many Christians is that they go on thinking they can bridge the gap by their own efforts, by their religious activities and good works, hoping they are doing enough to please God. But of course they can never be sure they have ever done enough to earn God's approval and forgiveness.

Jesus' death on the cross tells us that God loves us, accepts us as we are, and forgives our sins as we put our trust in Him. Jesus bore the full consequences of all human sin:

> *For Christ died for sins once for all, the righteous for the unrighteous, to bring you to God. He was put to death in the body but made alive by the Spirit.* 1 PETER 3:18

Forgiveness of our sins rests entirely on the finished work of Jesus on the cross. Just before He died Jesus cried out in a loud voice, "It is finished" (John 19:30). This was a shout of victory—"The work is done! The debt of man's sin is paid, finished, blotted out forever." We can never earn forgiveness. The Bible tells us that even our good works are like filthy rags compared to the absolute perfection of God.

The cross tells us that the enormous debt of our sin has been fully paid by Jesus Christ once and for all. When we accept Jesus into our lives, we receive God's forgiveness. Every sin we have ever done is blotted out forever.

> *As far as the east is from the west, so far has he removed our transgressions from us.*
> PSALM 103:12

God is able not only to forgive all our sins but to forget them, totally blot out of His memory all knowledge of them.

> *"For I will forgive their wickedness and will remember their sins no more."*
> JEREMIAH 31:34

You may well find this hard to understand and accept, but this is the measure of God's love for you.

One of the most beautiful illustrations of God's love and forgiveness is shown in Jesus' parable of the prodigal son. The younger son wants his father's money to live his life his own way. He wastes all of it, and when left with nothing, he remembers his father and determines to go home expecting to be disowned and punished. He is truly sorry. "I have sinned against heaven and against you. I am no longer worthy to be called your son" (Luke 15:21). But the father wraps his arms around him, gives him new clothes and a ring, the sign of his sonship. There is not one word of rebuke—just total acceptance and forgiveness.

Paul sums it up in these words:

> *To the praise of his glorious grace, which he has freely given us in the One he loves. In him we have redemption through his blood, the forgiveness of sins, in accordance with the riches of God's grace.*   EPHESIANS 1:6–7

I'M NOT PERFECT—
WHY DO I STILL SIN?

When we ask Jesus Christ into our lives, we become a son or daughter of God. We have begun a new life. We have been born again. God the Father fully accepts us and forgives us for Jesus' sake. He becomes our Father and we become His children. A new relationship between us and Him has been established that nothing can break.

This does not mean we suddenly become perfect. A criminal who has served his prison sentence is, in the eyes of the law, a free man. But he doesn't suddenly become perfect. He is the same person inside. But with the Christian there is a big difference. God gives us the Holy Spirit. Our aim now is not to please ourselves, but to please Jesus and to live for Him and to become like Him.

God has given us the Holy Spirit to do this work in us. But sadly we still sin, however hard we try. God has given us a new nature, but the old one will be with us until the day we die when it will be removed from us forever.

What happens if I sin? Do I have to ask Jesus into my life all over again? Will God reject me or disown me?

Imagine a boy playing football in the garden who kicks the ball right through a window and smashes it. He had been told not to play there with the football. He keeps out of the way. At mealtime there is an icy silence, for he knows he has disobeyed his father. This will last until he owns up and says he is sorry. The relationship has not changed; he is still a son; he doesn't have to ask to become a member of the family. He never ceases to be a son. It is the friendship that has been temporarily broken, until he says he is sorry.

When you disobey Christ, or are thoughtless or self-centered, when you do, say, or think something you know to be wrong, you are still a child of God. He doesn't disown you. The relationship has not changed—you do not have to be born again into God's family. You are in His family. You do not have to ask Jesus into your life again. He is already there. What you have done is to spoil the friendship with Him, and it is up to you to own up and say you're sorry and ask for His forgiveness. This is how the apostle John put it:

> *If we claim to be without sin, we deceive ourselves and the truth is not in us. If we confess our sins, he is faithful and just and will forgive us our sins and purify us from all unrighteousness.*   1 JOHN 1:8–9

THE GIFT OF THE HOLY SPIRIT

When you receive Jesus into your life, you receive the Holy Spirit. You cannot be a Christian without having the Holy Spirit. He is Jesus' personal representative in your life. Jesus' resurrection body is in heaven where He is at the place of all power and authority. While on earth He could only be at one place at a time. By sending the Holy Spirit, He can be with all Christians at all times and in all places. He promised,

> *"And surely I am with you always, to the very end of the age."*   MATTHEW 28:20

He has kept His promise by sending the Holy Spirit. His special work in the Christian is to assure us of God's love and to empower us in our service and witness.

He assures us that the gospel is true.

> *"When the Counselor comes, whom I will send to you from the Father, the Spirit of truth who goes out from the Father, he will testify about me."* JOHN 15:26

He assures us that we really are in Christ.

> *We know that we live in him and he in us, because he has given us of his Spirit.*
> 1 JOHN 4:13

He assures us that God is our Father.

> *For you did not receive a spirit that makes you a slave again to fear, but you received the Spirit of sonship. And by him we cry, "Abba, Father."* ROMANS 8:15

He assures us that we truly belong to God.

And do not grieve the Holy Spirit of God, with whom you were sealed for the day of redemption.   EPHESIANS 4:30

He assures us we are special in God's sight.

And hope does not disappoint us, because God has poured out his love into our hearts by the Holy Spirit, whom he has given us.
                                        ROMANS 5:5

Do you not know that your body is a temple of the Holy Spirit, who is in you, whom you have received from God?
                              1 CORINTHIANS 6:19

When doubts come, remind yourself:

- who you are: a sinner, yes, but saved by Christ.
- who you belong to: the Lord Jesus Christ, Lord of heaven and earth.
- who you have in you: God's Holy Spirit.
- what you are part of: the body of Christ, the church.

THE BODY OF CHRIST

It is quite true that as an individual you give your life to Christ. You personally trust in Him as your Savior and Lord. But you are not meant to be a kind of Robinson Crusoe, living on your own and having to rely on your own resourcefulness. When you trust in Christ you become one with Him, the head. But you also become one with His body, the church.

The church is not a building; it is not bricks and mortar and glass, pews, and organs. It is people, ordinary people from all countries and backgrounds, of all races, tribes, and languages, all cultures, colors, and classes who have this in common—they love Jesus and follow Him. The church is described in many ways in the Bible: God's own people, a holy nation, the army of God, the family of God, the flock of Christ, God's temple, the bride of Christ.

Perhaps the picture of the body is the most vivid one, the body of Christ. The church is permanently and perfectly joined to Christ the head, who directs and controls the whole body. (See 1

Corinthians 12). Not only are you as a Christian linked inseparably to Christ, and the Holy Spirit like the life-blood flows into you and through you, you are also joined to the other members.

Just as in a human body there are many parts, so also in Christ's body. We are all different. We each have a particular function. No one member is more important than the other. We each need each other if the body is to function properly. If one is hurting we all feel it and share it. Each is of infinite value, each has his or her own contribution and gifts.

It is this church against which, Jesus said, the gates of Hades cannot overcome (Matthew 16:18). It is this church, Paul said, that Christ gave Himself up for, to make her holy, cleansing her, in order to present her to Himself holy and blameless as a radiant church (Ephesians 5:25–27).

It is this church that is commissioned to proclaim the good news of Jesus to all people and make disciples.

It is this church that will be gathered from every part of the world at Christ's return, with not one member missing, to reign and live with Him in glory in heaven, gathering together all those still living and all those who have died in faith.

Make sure you are an active, committed member of the body of Christ where you live: Join a local church where the gospel is loved and preached, so that you may "grow up into him who is the Head, that is, Christ" (Ephesians 4:15).

BAPTISM INTO CHRIST

Baptism is the sign or mark of the Christian faith. Being baptized no more makes someone a Christian than wearing a ring makes someone married. The ring in marriage is the symbol that a couple are married. The man and the woman have made solemn promises to each other, a covenant between them has been made and the ring is the outward sign of this. Baptism is the outward sign that you have pledged your life to Jesus. It is the public acknowledgment that you have turned from your old way of life and put your trust in Jesus as your Lord and Savior.

It gives to the Christian great assurance that he or she is Christ's. In baptism you are acknowledging that Jesus is Lord. It is public testimony that you belong to Him. It marks your entrance into the family of God. It is the outward sign that you have been born again, that you are a child of God, a member of His body.

For we were all baptized by one Spirit into one body—whether Jews or Greeks, slave or free—and we were all given the one Spirit to drink.   1 CORINTHIANS 12:13

Baptism is like a visual aid of the gospel. It portrays Jesus' death and resurrection and shows the Christian's oneness with his Lord.

Or don't you know that all of us who were baptized into Christ Jesus were baptized into his death? We were therefore buried with him through baptism into death in order that, just as Christ was raised from the dead through the glory of the Father, we too may live a new life.   ROMANS 6:3–4

Baptism is like a symbolic burial of your old life, an end to the life of self. It is also the symbol of your new life in Christ, sharing His resurrection life. The apostle Paul put it so clearly:

I have been crucified with Christ and I no longer live, but Christ lives in me. The life I live in the body, I live by faith in the Son of God, who loved me and gave himself for me. GALATIANS 2:20

Baptism is a picture that every Christian has been cleansed from sin through Christ's death.

Let us draw near to God with a sincere heart in full assurance of faith, having our hearts sprinkled to cleanse us from a guilty conscience and having our bodies washed with pure water. HEBREWS 10:22

Baptism is a constant reminder of your new life in Christ and His gift of the Holy Spirit to dwell in you.

Baptism is the sign of your willingness to present your body to God as an instrument for His will and service.

Baptism is the signing on in the King's army;

it is a declaration of war against sin and evil and the devil.

THE LORD'S SUPPER

The first Lord's Supper took place on the last Thursday of Jesus' earthly life, just before Good Friday and His death on the cross. He met with His disciples to celebrate the Jewish Passover. This reminded the Jews of their amazing escape from slavery in Egypt centuries earlier. God's Angel of Death was going to destroy all the firstborn in the land. The Jews were told to sprinkle the blood of a perfect lamb over the doorposts of their houses and the angel would 'pass over' them.

Jesus gave this family meal, this Passover, a new and deeper meaning. He was the perfect lamb to be slain, His blood was to be sprinkled on the cross, so that God's judgment would pass over all who trust Him. This is how Paul describes it:

For I received from the Lord what I also passed on to you: The Lord Jesus, on the night he was betrayed, took bread, and when he had given thanks, he broke it and said, "This is my body, which is for you; do this in remembrance of me."

1 CORINTHIANS 11:23–24

The Lord's Supper proclaims the Lord's death by words and symbols. Christ's body is represented by the bread, His blood by the wine. The bread is broken and the wine poured out as a visual aid of Jesus' death on the cross. It is also called the Breaking of the Bread or Holy Communion to show our oneness with Jesus and with our fellow-Christians. It is sometimes called the Eucharist, which comes from the Greek word meaning "thanksgiving," because Jesus gave thanks when He took the bread and cup of wine. It is a memorial meal, to remind Christians of the center of our faith—the cross. As we share in it, we are sharing in Christ's death. It expresses our oneness with Christ and with our fellow-Christians as we share the bread and wine.

It assures us of His love in dying for us. It strengthens our faith as we see the symbols of His love before our eyes. We feed upon Him by faith. Jesus said:

> *"I am the bread of life. He who comes to me will never go hungry, and he who believes in me will never be thirsty."*   JOHN 6:35

The Lord's Supper looks ahead to the second coming of Jesus in glory, something to fill us with joy and hope and praise.

> *For whenever you eat this bread and drink this cup, you proclaim the Lord's death until he comes.*   1 CORINTHIANS 11:26

THE CERTAINTY OF
HIS COMING

A s I look out at the world I sometimes get really afraid.

Will we blow ourselves up? How is it all going to end?

Is God really in control? How can I be sure?

Will I go to heaven when I die?

The Bible tells us on page after page that God is the sovereign Lord of heaven and earth.

> *The LORD reigns, he is robed in majesty;*
> *the LORD is robed in majesty and is armed*
> *with strength. The world is firmly estab-*
> *lished; it cannot be moved. Mightier than*
> *the thunder of the great waters, mightier*
> *than the breakers of the sea—the LORD on*
> *high is mighty.*   PSALM 93:1, 4

Jesus said:

> *"All authority in heaven and on earth has*
> *been given to me."* MATTHEW 28:18

God's purpose for His world is slowly but surely
being worked out. Evil is still rampant, but the
day is fast coming when,

> *At the name of Jesus every knee should*
> *bow, in heaven and on earth and under*
> *the earth, and every tongue confess that*
> *Jesus Christ is Lord, to the glory of God the*
> *Father.* PHILIPPIANS 2:10–11

Jesus won the victory on the cross once and for
all. The devil, called Satan in the Bible as the
very personification of evil, is a defeated foe; his
time is short. The final destruction of all evil will
be when Jesus comes again. His promise is sure:

> *I will come back and take you to be with*
> *me that you also may be where I am.*
> JOHN 14:3

The New Testament is full of the certainty of Jesus' return in glory to end human history, to stop evil once and for all, to gather all His people into the heavenly kingdom He is preparing for them.

> *So we will be with the Lord forever.*
> I THESSALONIANS 4:17

Until that day there will be wars and suffering. God allows us our freedom of choice, and it is this that is the cause of the crime and evil and subsequent suffering. But God is active in His world. His grace and love are constantly calling people to turn to Him and trust Him. He is with His people in their pain and hurts. No suffering, no trouble of any kind can ever separate us from His love. (Read again Paul's triumphant words in Romans 8:35–39.)

A CERTAIN FUTURE

Illness and physical pain, tragedies, accidents, and death will come to Christians as to others simply because we are human. We will suffer because of other people's greed and selfishness, because we are part of society and what we do affects others for good and bad.

But God promises us a new body when we die, a resurrection body like Jesus' body. Just as a bird has a body for flying in the sky, the fish a body for living in the sea, and we have a body for living on earth, so when we die we shall be given a body just right for living in heaven. The apostle John wrote:

But we know that when he appears, we shall be like him, for we shall see him as he is.   1 JOHN 3:2

But thanks be to God! He gives us the victory through our Lord Jesus Christ.
                              1 CORINTHIANS 15:57

The Christian can face the world, life and all it throws at us, the future, even death itself, with total confidence—not in ourselves and our own strength and wisdom, but in our almighty, all-knowing, all-loving God.

> *To him who is able to keep you from falling and to present you before his glorious presence without fault and with great joy. . .*
> JUDE 24

> *You, dear children, are from God and have overcome them, because the one who is in you is greater than the one who is in the world.*
> 1 JOHN 4:4

> *No, in all these things we are more than conquerors through him who loved us.*
> ROMANS 8:37

As we let the Holy Spirit fill our lives, so we will experience the victorious life of Jesus in us, giving us an ever growing confidence in Him.

And we. . .are being transformed into his likeness with ever-increasing glory, which comes from the Lord, who is the Spirit.

2 CORINTHIANS 3:18

A certain faith. Yes, because it is rooted in God Himself.

I know I am a child of God, because He says so in the Bible.

God knows I am His child because He sees Jesus in me.

Others know I am because it shows in my life through the indwelling Holy Spirit.

Already He is at work making us more like Jesus, preparing us for the day when we shall see Him, be made like Him, and be with Him forever.

Inspirational Library

Beautiful purse/pocket-size editions of Christian classics bound in flexible leatherette. These books make thoughtful gifts for everyone on your list, including yourself!

When I'm on My Knees   The highly popular collection of devotional thoughts on prayer, especially for women.
    Flexible Leatherette $4.97

The Bible Promise Book   Over 1,000 promises from God's Word arranged by topic. What does God promise about matters like: Anger, Illness, Jealousy, Love, Money, Old Age, and Mercy? Find out in this book!
    Flexible Leatherette $3.97

Daily Wisdom for Women   A daily devotional for women seeking biblical wisdom to apply to their lives. Scripture taken from the New American Standard Version of the Bible.
    Flexible Leatherette $4.97

My Daily Prayer Journal   Each page is dated and features a Scripture verse and ample room for you to record your thoughts, prayers, and praises. One page for each day of the year.
    Flexible Leatherette $4.97

Available wherever books are sold.
Or order from:

Barbour Publishing, Inc.
P.O. Box 719
Uhrichsville, OH 44683
http://www.barbourbooks.com

If you order by mail, add $2.00 to your order for shipping.
Prices are subject to change without notice.